I0015334

Important note for users of this courseware:

This course is accompanied by additional course documents that can be downloaded for free. Once you have purchased the courseware, please contact the author below for a zip folder containing these files:

E-mail: ProfSkipLaratonda@gmail.com

Allegheny Valley Institute of Technology ®
Authorized Training Programs

About the author:

E. F. Laratonda has over forty years of experience related to analog and digital electrical design, computer and microprocessor-based product design, computer networking, information technology management and computer technology training. His career includes tenures with Texas Instruments, United Technologies, Westinghouse and the Pennsylvania State University. He has managed the design, configuration and administration of hundreds of client computers in both corporate and school district environments and has taught at both the community college and university levels. Presently, he teaches Electrical Engineering at Penn State and helps educate corporate "information technology" personnel in the areas of computer networking, security, operating systems and project management.

E. F. "Skip" Laratonda, MSEE, PE
Director/CEO, Allegheny Valley Institute
Microsoft Certified Systems Engineer
Microsoft Certified Trainer

Allegheny Valley Institute of Technology ®

Authorized Training Programs

Information in this document is subject to change without notice and does not represent a commitment on the part of **Allegheny Valley Institute of Technology**. Under the copyright laws, no part of this document may be copied, photocopied, reproduced, translated, or reduced to any electronic medium or machine-readable form, in whole or in part, without prior written consent of the **Allegheny Valley Institute of Technology**.

ISBN-13: 978-1725075436

ISBN-10: 1725075431

TABLE OF CONTENTS
VISUAL BASIC FOR APPLICATIONS, LEVEL I

Allegheny Valley Institute of Technology ®
Authorized Training Programs

Allegheny Valley Institute of Technology ®

Authorized Training Programs

Visual Basic for Applications
(Level I)

Introduction

Visual Basic is a descendant of **BASIC**, which has been around for several decades. **BASIC** (an acronym for *Beginners' All-Purpose Symbolic Instruction Code*) was originally developed at Dartmouth University in 1964 as a language for beginning programmers.

BASIC has developed, through the help of Xerox and Microsoft, into **Visual BASIC** which has evolved into an extremely powerful application development tool for the Windows environment. Since its introduction, **Visual BASIC** has gradually left its reputation as a beginners' language far behind and has become one of the most popular – and powerful – Windows programming languages.

Visual Basic is truly an evolutionary programming language. It combines procedural and structural programming with two innovative techniques that are revolutionizing the computer programming world:

    A. Object-oriented programming

    B. Event-driven programming

Allegheny Valley Institute of Technology ®
Authorized Training Programs

What is Object-Oriented Programming?

A person's interaction with everyday life consists of interfacing with **objects**, object **properties**, and actions (methods and events) pertaining to those objects. **Objects** have been assigned characteristics (**Properties**) that help define them and the actions express how we behave with these objects:

Object	Properties	Methods	Events
Car	Model, year, color	Drive, park	Driving, parking
Classroom	Size, floor, color	None	None
Marker	Size, color	Write	Writing
Eraser	Size, material, color	Erase	Erasing
Wastepaper basket	Size, material, color	None	None

Notice that while all objects have *properties*, they do not necessarily have *methods* or *events* associated with them.

From a programmer's point of view, objects are programs that are pre-defined:

- **Forms** - a window or dialog box
- **Controls** - buttons, labels, text boxes, check boxes, radio buttons, dropdown boxes, scroll bars etc.
- **System** related
    1. Desktop
    2. Task Bar
    3. Start Button
    4. Applications
    5. Clipboard
    6. Debug
    7. Printer
    8. Screen

Allegheny Valley Institute of Technology ®

Authorized Training Programs

The data are the **characteristics** (or *properties*) of an object and **procedures** (or *methods*) are its behaviors. You encapsulate an object's characteristics and its behaviors within a single block of source code. Characteristics and behaviors are in one place, physically (in the same block of code) and conceptually (in an object). Placing data and the operations to manipulate the data together is known as *encapsulation*.

Visual Basic saves time and effort by letting you reuse existing objects (applications or objects within applications). The **Visual Basic** programming system includes a library of existing objects you can use to interface directly with Windows. All the objects you need to get started are coded for you. You can use them as they exist or modify them by changing their properties or re-implementing their event procedures. In addition, you can extend the **Visual Basic** system by adding custom controls (VBX's or OCX's), linking to dynamic link libraries (DLLs), and manipulating and communicating with other applications through dynamic data exchange (DDE) and object linking and embedding (OL&E). These topics are discussed in detail in the Level II course in **Visual Basic**.

This **object-oriented** technique should be consistent with how you think about a Windows application. Each application running in a "Windows" window is an object that sends and receives messages. To accomplish a task, you must send a message to an application window (that is, to an object).

Allegheny Valley Institute of Technology ®

Authorized Training Programs

What is Event-Driven Programming?

Visual Basic is an *event driven* programming language. This means that *event procedure* code is executed as a response to an event. For example, if you click on an object (**Exit** button), the code that corresponds to this event is executed. The programmer's job is to write the appropriate code and attach it to the appropriate object and/or event. **Event-driven** programming languages are not always the best alternative, but with today's Windows applications it has enormous advantages over other techniques:

- Easy to Use
- Graphics Oriented
- Provides a common interface to Windows

The Microsoft **Visual Basic** programming system is an exciting step forward for anyone who is involved in writing Windows-based distributed Web applications. With its event-driven programming engine and innovative, easy-to-use visual design tools, Visual Basic lets you take full advantage of the Windows graphical environment to build powerful applications quickly.

The word **Basic** in **Visual Basic**. may be misleading. You might think that all serious Windows applications should be written using the C/C++ compiler and the SDK (software development kit) for Windows. However, this is not the case. After taking this Level I course, you will be able to write Windows programs in a fraction of the time that it takes to write the same programs using other programming languages.

As its name suggests, a big portion of the programming with **Visual Basic** is accomplished visually. This means that during *design time*, you are able to see how your program will look during *run time*. This is a great advantage over other programming languages, because you are able to change and experiment with your design until you are satisfied with the colors, sizes, and images that are included in your program.

This course assumes no prior experience in **Visual Basic**. So take your time and ask questions as the instructor covers the material.

Allegheny Valley Institute of Technology ®

Authorized Training Programs

Introduction to Visual Basic for Applications (VBA)

Microsoft's Access, Excel, Word and PowerPoint contain a powerful macro language called *Visual Basic for Applications (VBA)*.

Visual Basic for Applications (VBA) is a programming environment designed specifically for **Office** application macros. VBA has become the standard language for macro programming in the **Microsoft Office Suite**. The advantage of a common macro programming language means that no matter what application you use, you will only have to learn one set of commands and techniques.

The power of **VBA** will be demonstrated, but the most obvious advantage is that it is easier to use than most macro programming languages. If you are not an experienced programmer, **VBA** enables you to write or record macros and attach them to buttons either on the worksheet or on the *Ribbon*. You also can create dialog boxes by simply drawing the appropriate controls onto a *UserForm*. Of course, if you want to get the most out of **VBA**, you'll need to augment your user interface with the **programming code**.

Creating a macro, in virtually all computer applications, is simply a method of automating a task or a series of tasks into a single, user-defined, easily accessible command. The word macro is an abbreviated form of the word *macroinstruction* that is defined as a series of *microinstructions*. This terminology has been in use many years before the first Personal Computer was designed.

What is a Macro and When Do You Need Them?

Microsoft Excel, as part of its structure, has **macros** created and assembled in a logical fashion that are accessible through menus and icons. In similar ways, you too, can assemble and combine various functions, commands and keystrokes into programs that help you perform tasks better and faster.

A **macro** is a sequence of functions, commands and/or keystrokes that perform repetitive or tedious tasks with a single command. This command can be a keystroke, click of the mouse or triggered off a computer operation.

Allegheny Valley Institute of Technology ®

Authorized Training Programs

Only your imagination and the requirements that you are faced with limit the number of uses for **macros**. Some of the most common uses for **macros** are:

- Printing macros
- Data Entry macros
- Formatting macros
- Charting macros

The types of **macros** you can create fall into three basic categories:

Command Macros - Macros that are so helpful in your day-to-day use of an application that you want them available all the time, no matter what type of file (Access, Excel, PowerPoint or Word) you are working with.

Task-Specific Macros - Macros that aid in accomplishing a particular task or function and are only needed with certain types of files.

Full Application Macros - Macros that, when combined with custom menus, dialog boxes and toolbars, create a comprehensive, standalone application.

Command macros are the most common type of **macro**. They store sequences containing commands from the menu, as well as keystrokes and mouse actions. The code that defines the command macro is called a *Sub procedure* or *procedure* for short. You activate command macros by clicking a button or pressing a Ctrl+key combination that you define or by choosing the macro name from a list box. You can also run command macros from custom menus and icons that you create. Command macros can range from the simple, such as worksheet formatting, to the complex, such as industry-specific applications with custom menus, help windows and dialog boxes.

Allegheny Valley Institute of Technology ®

Authorized Training Programs

Understanding and Creating Command Macros

There are two ways to create command **macros**:

- Use the built-in **macro recorder**
- Write the **Visual Basic** code

Recording is the simplest way to create a macro. The **macro recorder** records keystrokes, commands, dialog check box states and mouse action selections and translates these actions into the appropriate **Visual Basic** statements. These statements are stored invisibly in *projects* within the workbook. The only way to see the **VBA** code is by using the **Visual Basic Editor**.

Writing **VBA macro code** is more complex but gives you much more control over the **macro** you are creating.

Allegheny Valley Institute of Technology ®
Authorized Training Programs

The VBA Interface

The **Developer** tab in **Excel** allows power users to utilize automation functions such as macros and allows you to develop applications using **forms** and **controls** within **Excel**.

Exercise #1: Getting Familiar with the Visual Basic Editor

1. Open **Microsoft Excel** and open a blank workbook.
2. Right-click anywhere on the **Ribbon** and choose **Customize the Ribbon.**
3. In the right side of the **Excel Options** dialog box under the **Main Tabs** section, put a check to the left of the **Developer** then click **OK**. This will add the **Developer** tab to the **Ribbon**.
4. Under the **Developer** tab in the **Code** group, click the **Visual Basic** button and the **Microsoft Visual Basic Editor** window will appear:

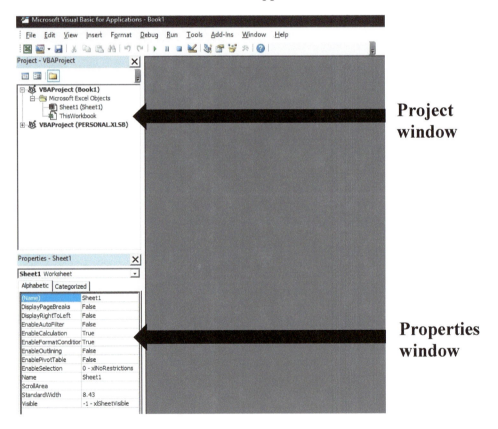

Notice the **Project** and **Properties** windows are on the left side!

Allegheny Valley Institute of Technology ®
Authorized Training Programs

5. On the **Menu,** click **Insert** and choose **UserForm**.

Notice how the interface changes:

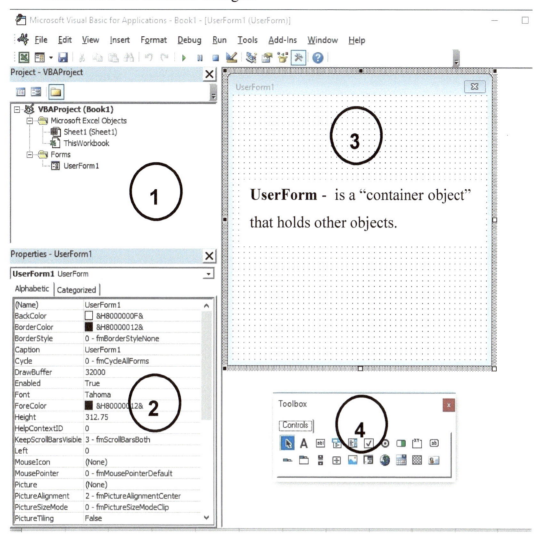

After you have inserted a **UserForm**, four different windows appear on the screen:

1. **Project** window
2. **Properties** window
3. **UserForm** window
4. **Toolbox** window

On your initial **UserForm** screen, the windows will overlap in the screen above, the windows have been resized and repositioned so that all of them can be seen together.

Allegheny Valley Institute of Technology ®

Authorized Training Programs

Creating Controls on the UserForm Window

UserForms are used to store the visual elements of an application along with any related *code pages*. Code pages contain the code that acts upon the form or any of the *controls* placed on the form. You can use *controls* to get user input and to display output. A *control* can be a command button, a data entry text box, or any number of other visual objects, but each control type responds to events, for which you must write code. Both forms and controls have *properties*, which describe the location, appearance and behavior of the form or control. You may set properties at design time in the *Properties window* or use the code to set them at run time.

Standard Controls in Visual Basic

The Toolbox Window

The *Toolbox*, contains the assortment of **visual controls** that you can select for use in your application. Each **control type** is represented by an icon in the *Toolbox*:

Identify each of the following tools on the toolbox shown below:

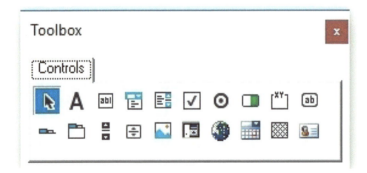

Allegheny Valley Institute of Technology ®

Authorized Training Programs

Learning how to use controls successfully is one of the most important aspects of developing **Excel** custom applications. For now, let's take a brief look at some of the **standard controls** represented in the **Toolbox** and review the purpose of each control.

1. Pointer

This is actually not a control at all, but rather represents the mouse pointer you use to select object.

2. Label

Labels are typically short strings of text that identify an element of a dialog box or display longer blocks of text.

3. Text Box

Text boxes are used to display code-generated text or to receive keyboard input from the user. Text boxes may be multiline capable, in which case they can perform automatic word wrapping. The **Text** property of a text box returns the box's contents in string form.

4. Combo Box

Combo boxes combine the features of a text box and a list box control. The **Style** property of a combo box allows you to select one of three styles:

- o *Drop-down combo*, which includes a drop-down list and an edit area.
- o *Simple-combo*, which includes an edit area and a list that is always displayed.
- o *Drop-down list*, which allows only selection from the drop-down list.

5. List Box

List box controls display a list of items from which the user may select one. The **List** property is a string array of the text items in the list. The **ListIndex** property indicates which item in the list is selected. The **ListCount** property returns the number of rows in the list.

Allegheny Valley Institute of Technology ®

Authorized Training Programs

6. Check Box

Check boxes provide the user with a Yes/No, Include/Exclude binary option.

When the option is selected, the check box displays a large . Unselected, the box is clear. **Check boxes** differ from **option buttons** in that more than one check box in a frame may be selected at one time.

7. Option Button

Sometimes referred to as a **radio button**, an option button is used to select one (and only one) option out of a group of two or more options. Selecting a button cancels the previous choice selected within the same group.

8. Frame

The **Frame** control provides a visual and functional grouping for related controls. If the frame is moved, all the controls within it move also. Option buttons placed within a frame acts as a group, i.e., only one option button at a time may be selected.

9. Command button

Command buttons, sometimes called *push buttons*, are used to execute a specific action when the user activates them.

10. TabStrip

The **TabStrip** acts like the dividers in a notebook or the labels on a group of file folders. By using a **TabStrip** control, you can define multiple pages for the same area of a window or dialog box in your application.

11. MultiPage

The **MultiPage** control is a container for a collection of Page objects. Each Page object contains its own set of controls and does not necessarily rely on other Page objects for information.

Allegheny Valley Institute of Technology ®

Authorized Training Programs

12. Scroll Bar

Scroll Bars depict a physical position or numerical quantity in relation to minimum and maximum values. Arrows appear on the ends of the bar, and a scroll box moves back and forth between the arrows to indicate relative position or value.

13. Spin Button

A **Spin** button can be used to increment a number in a cell.

14. Image

This control is used to display bitmaps, icons or **Windows** metafiles. It acts like a **command** button when clicked.

After you have read page 14, create the following **User Interface**:

How many "objects" do you see?

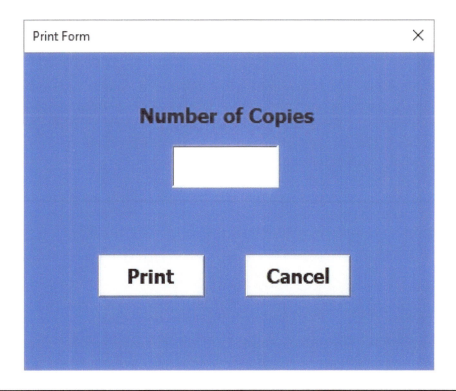

Allegheny Valley Institute of Technology ®
Authorized Training Programs

Object Naming Conventions (very important)

When you first create a form or control *object*, **Visual Basic** assigns its **Name** property a default value, such as **UserForm1**, **CommandButton2** or **TextBox3**. It is good programming practice to change such objects' names to more descriptive names that describe each object's function and type. For example, a **UserForm1** object might be named **frmInventoryList**; and a **TextBox3** control might be called **txtPartNumber**. In each case, a prefix identifies the type of object, and the remainder of the name identifies the object's function or purpose.

When using VBA, the first three characters of the **Name** property of objects are **very important**. When a programmer assigns an object a name, the first three letters indicate what type of *object* **VBA** is dealing with. Here is a partial list:

frm	UserForm objects
cbo	Combo box
chk	Check box objects
cmd	Command button objects
hsb	Horizontal scroll bar objects
lbl	Label objects
txt	Text box objects
vsb	Vertical scroll bar

Before we continue, remember that a *userform* is an *object* and *objects* have characteristics called *properties*. The *Caption* is just one of the many properties of a userform. As you can see from the **Properties** window the form has many other properties. As an example select the "BackColor" property from the **Properties** list. Select the down arrow to the right of the settings box. Choose a form background color for your design.

Note(s): It is good programming practice to assign names to **objects** before you begin **writing code.** Therefore, assign the name immediately after you place the object.

Name Property ≠ Caption Property

The **Name** is used by the programmer for code referencing.

The **Caption** is for the end user. It is what is visible on the interface!

Allegheny Valley Institute of Technology ®

Authorized Training Programs

Designing and Building Applications with VBA

Writing **VBA** programs involves two steps:

      1st   a ***visual programming*** step

      2nd   a ***code programming*** step

During the ***visual programming*** step, you design your program with the tools that come with the **VBA** system. You do not have to write code. You simply place, size and define objects.

In the ***code programming*** step, you write program procedures using a text editor.
The programs are composed of statements written in the **VBA** programming language.
Programming is simplified with **VBA**, but a logical thinking process on behalf of the programmer is a must.

Creating Your First Program

Before we begin your first exercise, create a directory that you will use to save your program files during the course of this class:

      Create a folder called "**VBA Class**" on your desktop.

Short-cut keys to use in this course:

Control + X   **cut**

Control + C   **copy**   **or just highlight the text and right-click on it.**

Control + V   **paste**

Control + Z   **undo**

Also, under **Tools/Options** put a check mark in the box for
Require Variable Declaration

Allegheny Valley Institute of Technology ®
Authorized Training Programs

Exercise #2 The Name Identification Program

The Specification:

Write a **VBA macro** called "**The Name Identification Program**" that will display the following window when started:

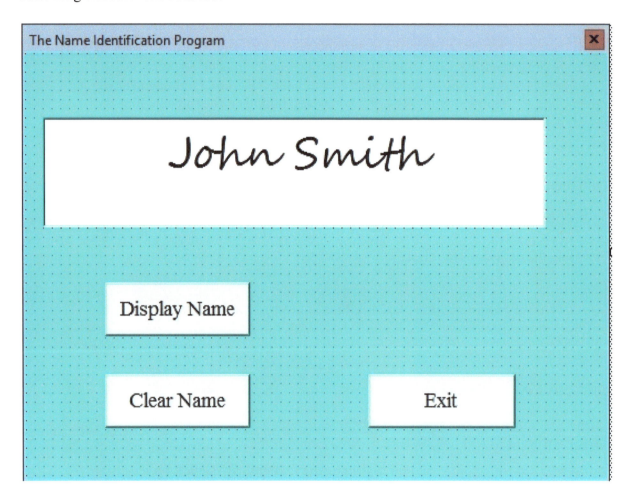

How many "objects" do you see above?

The **userform** will be comprised of "3" **command** buttons and a **text** box as shown above. When you click the **Display Name** button, your name will be displayed in the **text box**. When you click the **Clear Name** button, your name will disappear from the **text box**. When you click on the **Exit** button, the macro will terminate.

Allegheny Valley Institute of Technology ®
Authorized Training Programs

Use the following steps to create a new project file for the **Name** program:

1. Start **Excel** and open a blank workbook.

2. Under the **Developer** tab in the **Code** group, click the **Visual Basic** button and the **Microsoft Visual Basic Editor** window will appear.

On the **Menu,** click **Insert** and choose **UserForm**.

Re-arrange and re-size the windows to look like:

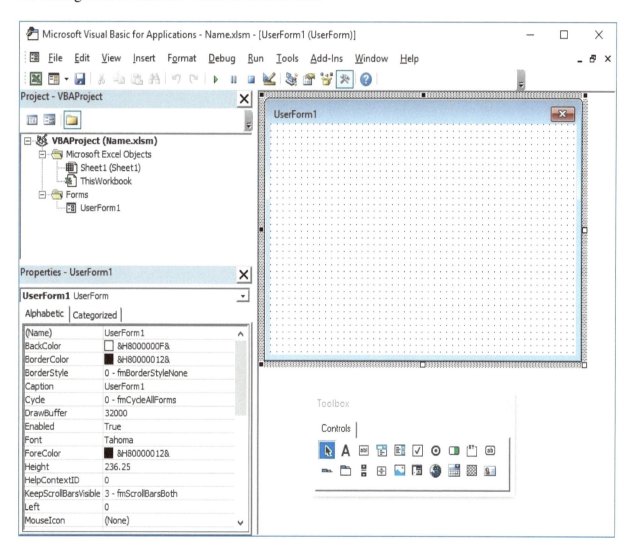

Allegheny Valley Institute of Technology ®
Authorized Training Programs

Examining the Project Window

Your **VBAProject** is called **Name.xlsx** and it consists of a single sheet and a single **userform**.

As your project gets more complicated, the number of **userforms** in this window will increase. To view the **Project** window, select **View/Project Explorer** from the **Menu** bar or click on the **Project** window.

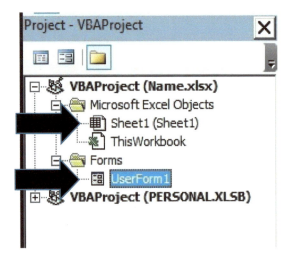

Allegheny Valley Institute of Technology ®

Authorized Training Programs

The Visual Programming Phase

Creating the User Interface

The **user interface** is perhaps the most important part of an application; it's certainly the most visible. To users, the interface is the application; they probably are not even aware of the code that is executed behind the controls. No matter how much time and effort you put into writing and optimizing your code, the usability of your application depends on the interface.

When you design an application, a number of decisions need to be made regarding the interface. Should you use the single-document or multiple-document style? How many different forms will you need? What commands will your menus include, and will you use toolbars to duplicate menu functions? What about dialog boxes to interact with the user? How much assistance do you need to provide?

The intended audience should also influence your design. An application aimed at a beginning user demands simplicity in its design, while one for experienced users may be more complex. Other applications used by your target audience may influence their expectations for an application's behavior. If you plan on distributing internationally, language and culture must be considered as part of your design.

Allegheny Valley Institute of Technology ®

Authorized Training Programs

Changing the Look of UserForms

When you add a new userform to your project, you are presented with a plain gray square box. As you add controls to your form, you change its appearance. However, there are a lot of changes you can make to the userform itself to make it more interesting and useable.

Here are a few **form** properties to investigate:

- Name
- BackColor
- BorderStyle
- Caption
- Height
- Left
- Top
- Width

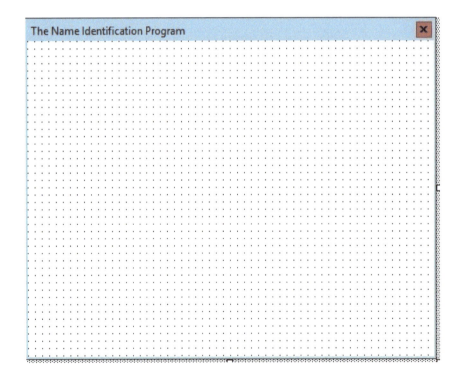

Allegheny Valley Institute of Technology ®

Authorized Training Programs

Changing the Caption Property of the UserForm

The blank **userform** that was created by **VBA** has the title "**UserForm1**". This default title should be changed to a more descriptive title. To change the title:

1. Select the **userform** by clicking on it.

2. In the **Properties** window, double-click the **Caption** item in the **Properties** list.

4. In the settings box of the **Properties** windows type:

   The Name Identification Program

5. Press **Enter**.

You have just changed the **Caption** property of the **userform**. Notice the new caption!!

Changing the Name Property of the UserForm

Each object in **VBA** must have a name. The name of the *object* is defined in the **Name** property in the **Properties** list. To change the **Name** property of the userform:

1. Select the *userform* by clicking anywhere on it.

2. In the **Properties window**, double-click the **Name** property.

3. In the **Settings** box of the **Properties window**, type **frmMain**

4. Press the **Enter** key.

5. **STOP** and wait for the instructor!

Allegheny Valley Institute of Technology ®

Authorized Training Programs

Save Your Work!

Select **File/Save** and the following message will appear:

You must click **NO** to the following message!

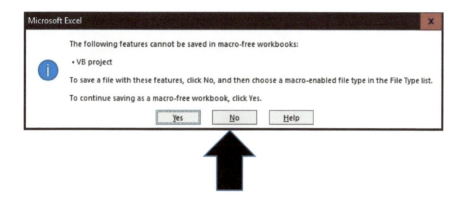

Because the workbook has a macro embedded in it, you must save it as an
Excel Macro-Enabled Workbook or you will lose the macro interface you created!

Select **File/Save** again and save the workbook in the **VBA Class** folder you created on the
desktop as "**NAME**" but this time as an:

Excel Macro-Enabled Workbook

Allegheny Valley Institute of Technology ®

Authorized Training Programs

Adding the Exit Button to the frmMain Form

As shown at the beginning of this exercise on page 14, the userform should have three **command** button objects on it: **Display Name**, **Clear Name** and **Exit**.

To place a **command button** inside your form, you have to pick it up from the **Tool box** window. The **Tool box** window is the window that contains **control objects**. You will pick up an object by clicking on it in the **tool box**. You will place the object on the form by **clicking** on the selected control object and drawing it on the form.

To place the **Exit** button inside the form:

1. Click on the **Command** button control ( ) in the **Tool box**. It is the fifth button in the second column.

2. Draw the Command button anywhere on the userform.

Default properties are assigned to the button, but we will be changing some of the properties on the next two pages, such as:

- Name
- Text
- Height, Left, Top and Width (location)
- Font

Allegheny Valley Institute of Technology ®

Authorized Training Programs

Changing the Name, Text, Location and Font Properties of the Exit button

Select the **Properties** window for the **Exit** button. Make sure the **Object** box displays **CommandButton1** and make the following edits to the properties list:

1. Change the **Name** property of **CommandButton1** from **CommandButton1** to **cmdExit**. Note the **cmd** prefix to the **Name** property.

2. Change the **Caption** property of **cmdExit** from **CommandButton1** to **Exit**.

3. Change the location of the **Exit** button by dragging it to the desired location. To drag the button, click anywhere inside the button and without releasing the left mouse button move the mouse. Notice that moving the location of the button changes the **Left** and **Top** properties in the **Property** window.

4. Change the **Font** property of the **cmdExit** button to **Times New Roman** and the **Font** (point size) to 14 point.

Note: One of the main advantages of **VBA** programming is that you instantly see the results of your visual programming.

Adding the Display Name and Clear Buttons to the frmMain UserForm

Placing the remaining buttons:

1. Add the **Display Name** button to the form by clicking the **CommandButton** control. Draw it in its defined location (see final design window) and resize it.

2. Add the **Clear Name** button to the form by clicking the **CommandButton** control. Draw it in its defined location (see final design window) and resize it.

Allegheny Valley Institute of Technology ®

Authorized Training Programs

Changing the Name, Caption and Font properties of the buttons

1. Change the **Name** property of the top **command** button to **cmdDisplay**.
2. Change the **Caption** property to **Display Name**.
3. Change the **Font** property to **Times New Roman**.
4. Change the **Font (point size)** property to 14 point.
5. Change the **Name** property of the bottom command button to **cmdClear**.
6. Change the **Caption** property to **Clear Name**.
7. Change the **Font** property to **Times New Roman**.
8. Change the **Font (point size)** property to 14 point.

Adding the Text Box Object to the frmMain UserForm

There is one more object to add to the form: the text box object. Place the text box inside the form:

1. Click on the text box tool ( ) in the **Tool bar** window and draw it on the userform. It is the second icon in the first column.
2. Move and resize the text box until it looks like the text box shown in the final design.
3. Change the **Name** property of the text box to **txtName**.
4. Change the **Font (name)** property to **Segoe Script**
5. Change the **Font (point size)** property to 28 point.
6. The default **TextAlign** property of the text box is 1-left justify. Because we want the text to appear in the middle of the text box, change the **TextAlign** property to 2-center.

Note: The **MultLine** property allows VBA to display more than one line in the text box.

The "visual programming" portion of the design is now complete.

Save Your Work!!

Allegheny Valley Institute of Technology ®

Authorized Training Programs

Building UserForms from Property Tables

Throughout this class you will not build userforms in the same way that you were instructed in **Exercise #2**. Instead you will be building the userform by looking at the completed userform and following a **Properties Table**. A **Properties Table** is a table that contains all the objects that are included on the userform, as well as all the properties that are different from the default properties. The following table is the **Properties Table** for the **Name Identification** program:

Object	Property	Setting
UserForm	**Name**	**frmMain**
	Caption	The Name Identification Program
Command Button	**Name**	**cmdExit**
	Caption	Exit
	Font	Times New Roman
	Font	14 (point size)
Command Button	**Name**	**cmdDisplay**
	Caption	Display Name
	FontName	Times New Roman
	FontSize	14 (point size)
Command Button	**Name**	**cmdClear**
	Caption	Clear Name
	Font	Times New Roman
	Font	14 (point size)
Text Box	**Name**	**txtName**
	Text	(nothing)
	Font	Segoe Script
	Font	28 (point size)
	TextAlign	2-Center

The Code Programming Phase

Attaching Visual Basic Code to the Objects

Before we begin!!

A Comment about Flowcharting

A **Flowchart** is a visual aid that lets the programmer see how and when instructions (functions) are executed during a program run. Flowcharting is a highly recommended intermediate step between the program specification and the actual writing of the **Visual Basic** code. Remarkably, it has been observed that perhaps 10% of the programmers can write a program successfully without having to flowchart. Unfortunately, it has also been noted that 90% of the programmers believe they belong to this 10%. In short, most novice programmers seldom see the necessity of drawing a flowchart. This usually results in erroneous programs. They must then spend unnecessary time testing their program (this is called the debugging phase). The practice of flowcharting is therefore a highly recommended procedure before writing the program code.

A Comment about Documenting a Program

Documenting your code is one of the most neglected, but necessary, part in the programming procedure. Documenting the code, with good comments, makes the code easier to understand. Months, week or days later, when you need to modify your code or understand someone else's code, you will be glad the comments are there.

Remember that **Visual Basic** is an *event driven* programming language. This means that code is executed as a response to an event. For example, when you click on the **Exit** button you would expect code to be executed that would exit the program. We will now begin the *code programming* step of the **Name Identification** program.

Allegheny Valley Institute of Technology ®

Authorized Training Programs

Attaching Code to the Exit Button

1. Double click on the **Exit** button. **Visual Basic** responds by displaying the **Code** window for the **Exit** button:

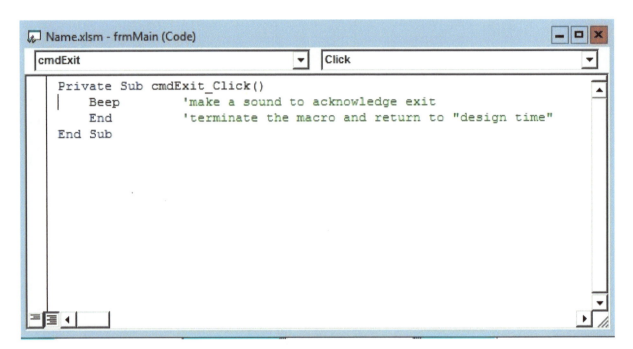

The command code that causes **Visual Basic** to terminate is ***End***. So type ***End*** between the *Private Sub* and *End Sub* statements as shown below. Sub is a command that must begin a **Visual Basic** *procedure*. A ***procedure*** is Visual Basic Code dedicated for a particular event. Just for fun let's make the program beep when it exits. To do this, type the command **Beep** before the *End* command.

Allegheny Valley Institute of Technology ®

Authorized Training Programs

Visual Basic Rules

The code is written in **Visual Basic** and follows the standard **Visual Basic** rules:

1. *Comments* begin with an apostrophe (') mark.

2. *Procedures* begin with the word *Sub*, followed by the name of the procedure.

3. *Procedures* end with the words *End Sub*.

4. The main body of the *procedure* consists of the *code* that does all the work. This *code* consists of a series of statements that command the program to perform the steps in the procedure.

Visual Basic is a color-coded programming language such that:

Blue	denotes *keywords* used by Visual Basic
Black	denotes commands
Green	denotes comments, used for documenting your code
Red	denotes syntax errors

Allegheny Valley Institute of Technology ®

Authorized Training Programs

What is a VBA Procedure?

- The word **Macro** is slang for the word **VBA procedure**. It is a throw back to pre 1994 **Microsoft Excel**

- A **procedure** is defined as a named group of statements that are run as a unit

  - A statement is simply 1 complete line of code

- **VBA procedures** are used to perform tasks such as controlling Excel's environment, communicating with databases, calculating equations, analyzing worksheet data, creating charts…etc

- A **VBA procedure** unit or block consists of a procedure statement (**Sub** or **Function**) and an ending statement with statements in between

- A **VBA procedure** is constructed from three types of statements: executable, declaration and assignment statements. The statements between a procedure's declaration and ending statement (i.e. **Sub** and **End Sub**) perform the procedure's task; what you are trying do.

- **Procedures** are typed and stored in a **Module**

- **Procedures** are executed or run in order to carry out their statements. When a procedure is run, its statements (i.e. lines) are executed in a top-down line by line fashion performing operations. Think of reading a book page. Note that typing a procedure in a module does not run it. You must do this after typing it by variety of different methods. Until you run it, it is just basically text sitting in a document.

- **VBA** has two basic types of procedures that you can create: **Sub procedures** and **Function procedures**

Allegheny Valley Institute of Technology ®

Authorized Training Programs

What is a **Sub Procedure**?

Sub procedures are written when you want to command Excel like creating a chart, analyzing data, coloring cells, copying and pasting data...etc. A simple Sub procedure is pictured below.

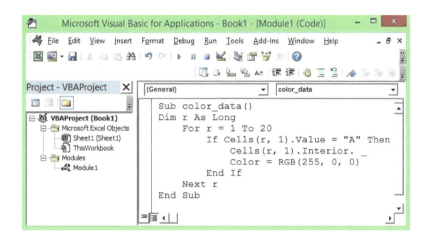

What is a VBA **Function Procedure**?

Function procedures are created when you want to make your own custom worksheet functions or perform a calculation that will be used over and over again in your computer code. Note that Sub procedures can also be used to do calculations. A simple function procedure is pictured below.

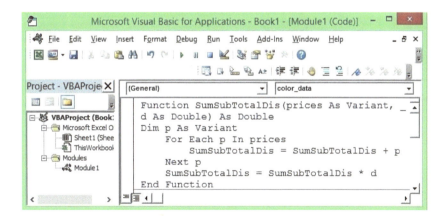

Allegheny Valley Institute of Technology ®

Authorized Training Programs

Scope of Procedures

When you create a *procedure*, you might want to limit where it can be called from (used) and how resources are allocated to make its code available to other parts of your custom application. The *scope* of a procedure refers to its availability to be used by other parts of your program code, and is determined by the context in which it is declared. *Scope* is also known as *visibility*.

A procedure's scope is determined by how it is defined. A procedure's scope can be defined one of two ways:

1. Private Procedures
2. Public Procedures

Private Procedures for a specific form or module (default)

Using the *Private* keyword in the **Sub** statement allows a procedure to be accessed only from the userform or module in which it is defined. This approach, of course, poses both advantages and disadvantages. One advantage is that you can have private procedures of the same name in different forms or modules. A disadvantage of course is that the procedure is not accessible from other forms or modules.

Public Procedures that can be used anywhere in the program

If you want to have your procedure to be accessible from any userform or module in your program, use the *Public* keyword when you define the procedure. Using the *Public* keyword allows a procedure defined in one form or module to be called from any other userform or module within a project. It also means that you have to be more careful with the names of your procedures because each *Public* procedure must have a unique name.

Note: If you omit the keywords *Public* and *Private* from the **Sub** statement, the procedure is set up by default as a **Public** procedure.

Allegheny Valley Institute of Technology ®

Authorized Training Programs

Assigning Values to the Properties of Objects (very important)

Syntax:

ObjectName . Property = Value

Attaching code to the **Display Name** and **Clear Name** buttons

1. Double-click on the **Display Name** button.
2. After the **Sub** statement, type   **txtName.Text = "Your Name"**
3. Double-click on the **Clear Name** button.
4. After the **Sub** statement, type   **txtName.Text = ""**

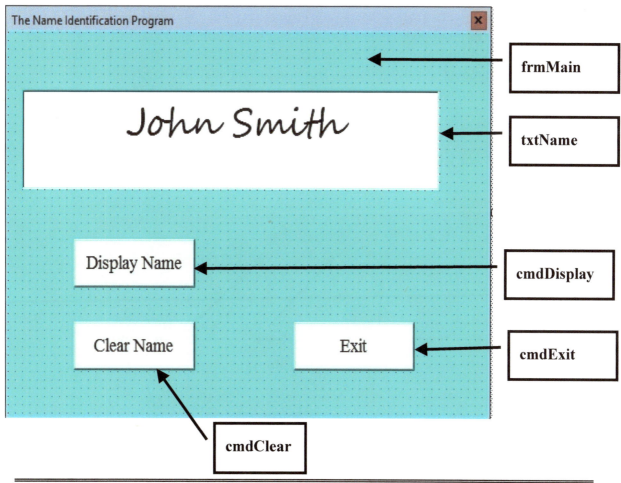

Allegheny Valley Institute of Technology ®
Authorized Training Programs

Save Your Work!

Running the Name Program

You have just completed the design of the **Name Identification** program. Before running it, make sure you have saved your work. To run the program, you need to execute **Visual Basic's Run Macro** command using any of the following methods:

- Choose **Run**/**Run Macro** from the **Menu** bar.
- Click the **Run Macro** button on the Visual Basic **Debug** toolbar.
- Press the **F5** function key at the top of the keyboard

When you execute the **Run Macro** command, **Visual Basic** compiles your program to check for certain types of errors; if your **Output** window is visible, you will see the results as it builds the application. If no errors are found, the program will begin executing and you will see your user interface. Notice in **Visual Basic's** title bar that you have gone from *design time* to *run time*, meaning that the program is actually running. Because the application is object-oriented and event-driven, it is waiting for you (the user) to cause an event to occur to an object, such as clicking a button.

The Debugging Tool Bar

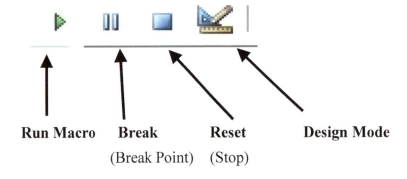

Run Macro   Break   Reset   Design Mode

(Break Point)   (Stop)

Allegheny Valley Institute of Technology ®

Authorized Training Programs

Review of the steps involved in Macro Program Design

1. Start with a written "specification". You need a specification that describes (in detail) the scope of the work to be performed.

2. Create the user interface by placing objects on the form.

3. Name the objects as you place them using an acceptable naming convention.

4. Set the "properties" of objects. (These are called the "initial conditions")

5. Prepare a step-by-step procedure to implement the code design. This is called the **algorithm**.

6. Draw a **Flow Chart** for each code procedure (if applicable) from the algorithm.

7. Write "event procedural code" (from the flow chart) for the objects by double-clicking on the objects.

Allegheny Valley Institute of Technology ®
Authorized Training Programs

Working with Event Procedures

How Event-Oriented Programming Works

In **Visual Basic**, an event is an action recognized by an object. For example, clicking the mouse or pressing a key is an event. In addition, the system can generate events (a timer event, for example). Event procedures are specific to objects. For example, when the object was **cmdExit** you wanted to define an action that responds to a user clicking the mouse on the **Exit** button. The default event procedure for a **CommandButton** was the **Click** event with the format:

> Sub cmdExit_Click ()

Or in general for any object:

> ObjectName_EventProcedure

Double click on the **Exit** button to view the *cmdExit* procedure. Change the **event** procedure to a *MouseMove* procedure. Notice that the first line of the procedure that **Visual Basic** automatically writes is different from the first line of the **Click** event procedure. Copy the **Click** procedural code into the **MouseMove** procedure and run the program.

Delete the MouseMove procedure.

Exercise #3   Working with Different Event Procedures

Using the knowledge you have learned so far, how could you "draw focus" to each button by making the caption of the button "bold" when you move the mouse pointer on it?

We will discuss different procedures at a later time.

<u>Save Your Work!</u>

Allegheny Valley Institute of Technology ®
Authorized Training Programs

Working with and Declaring Variables

Your **VBA** procedures often will need to store temporary values for use in later statements and calculations. *Variables* are used to store these values in the computer's memory while your programs are running. For example, you might want to store values for **total sales** and **total expenses** to use later in a **gross profit** calculation. In **Visual Basic**, as in most programming languages, you store temporary values in *variables*. Three components define a variable:

1. The variable's name
2. The type of information being stored in the variable
3. The actual information contained in the variable

Declaring a variable tells **Visual Basic** the name of the variable you are going to use. You declare variables by including *Dim* statements (**Dim** is short for dimension) at the beginning of each *Sub* or *Function* procedure:

Dim *variableName* [As type]

Some examples are:

> **Dim**   intAge As **Integer**
>
> **Dim**   bytPressure As **Byte**
>
> **Dim**   decSales, decExpenses As **Decimal**
>
> **Dim**   dblTemperature As **Double** = 98.6

Using the lower case, 3 letter prefix in the name is just an agreed-upon way of assigning variable names so you can tell more about them. The name must begin with an alphabetic character with no more than 40 characters, it can't be a **Visual Basic** keyword (Sub, Now, End etc..), it can't contain a space or begin with any of the following characters:

> . ! # $ % & @

Allegheny Valley Institute of Technology ®

Authorized Training Programs

Visual Basic supports implicit declarations, and it does not force you to declare the variable with a **Dim** statement. This means that if it sees a name it doesn't recognize, it assumes that the name belongs to a new variable. If you have experience with other programming languages, you probably know that some programming languages, like **Visual Basic**, do not require you to declare variables.

However, it is a good programming habit to declare all variables to avoid typing errors.
As an example:

> *Time1 = 10*
>
> *Speed1 = 50*
>
> *Distance = Speed1 * Time1*
>
> *MsgBox "Distance = " &* ==**Distnce**==

Now suppose, in error, you typed in **Distnce** and forgot the "a". Visual Basic considers **Distnce** as a new variable, and automatically assigns the value 0 to it. Thus, the **MsgBox** function displays the following:

> *Distance = 0*

You avoid this problem by declaring your variables:

> **Dim** *Time 1*   As   **Integer**
>
> **Dim** *Speed1*   As   **Integer**
>
> **Dim** *Distance* As   **Long**

To instruct **Visual Basic** to complain whenever there is a variable in the code that is not declared, place the following statement inside the general declarations section of the form:

> **Option Explicit**

NOTE:

> Putting a check in the **Require Variable Declaration** box under **Tools/Options/Editor** in the **Visual Basic Editor**, forces **Visual Basic** to add the *Option Explicit* statement at the beginning of each new code sheet (UserForm or Module). This statement will tell **Visual Basic** to generate an error whenever it comes across a variable name that hasn't been declared explicitly with a **Dim, Static or Public** statement.

Allegheny Valley Institute of Technology ®

Authorized Training Programs

Visual Basic Variable Data Types

Declaring variable data types helps to eliminate errors, reduce the size of compiled code and increase execution time. The data type of a variable determines the kind of data the variable can hold. Below is a list of **VBA** data types:

Data type	Storage size	Range
Byte	1 byte	0 to 255
Boolean	2 bytes	**True** or **False**
Integer	2 bytes	-32,768 to 32,767
Long (long integer)	4 bytes	-2,147,483,648 to 2,147,483,647
Single (single-precision floating-point)	4 bytes	-3.402823E38 to -1.401298E-45 for negative values; 1.401298E-45 to 3.402823E38 for positive values
Double (double-precision floating-point)	8 bytes	-1.79769313486231E308 to -4.94065645841247E-324 for negative values; 4.94065645841247E-324 to 1.79769313486232E308 for positive values
Currency (scaled integer)	8 bytes	-922,337,203,685,477.5808 to 922,337,203,685,477.5807
Decimal	14 bytes	+/-79,228,162,514,264,337,593,543,950,335 with no decimal point; +/-7.9228162514264337593543950335 with 28 places to the right of the decimal; smallest non-zero number is +/-0.0000000000000000000000000001
Date	8 bytes	January 1, 100 to December 31, 9999
Object	4 bytes	Any **Object** reference
String (variable-length)	10 bytes + string length	0 to approximately 2 billion
String (fixed-length)	Length of string	1 to approximately 65,400
Variant (with numbers)	16 bytes	Any numeric value up to the range of a **Double**
Variant (with characters)	22 bytes + string length	Same range as for variable-length **String**

Allegheny Valley Institute of Technology ®

Authorized Training Programs

Working with and Declaring Constants

Creating User-Defined Constants

To create your own constant, use the **Const** statement:

Syntax:

Const *CONSTANTNAME = expression*

CONSTANTNAME	The name of the constant. Most programmers use all uppercase names for constants.
expression	The value (or a formula that returns a value) that you want to use for the constant.

For example, the following statement creates a constant named **PI** and assigns it a value of **3.141593**

Const PI = 3.141593

Scope of Variables

Like **procedures**, variables also have **scope**. They can be local to a specific procedure, available to an entire userform, or available to the entire program. Again, the **scope** depends on where the variable is defined and which keyword is used in its declaration.

You have more choices for the **scope** of variables than for the scope of procedures. The **scope** is dependent not only on the keyword used to declare the variable but also on the location of the declaration statement.

The scope of a variable is determined at the time the variable is declared. In **Microsoft VBA**, the three scopes available for variables are procedure, module, and public.

Procedure (local) scope

To keep a variable private to a specific procedure, the variable must be declared in that procedure. (The keywords are **Dim** and **Static**)

Procedure variables only exist while the procedure is running. When the procedure terminates, the memory used for the variable is released and the value of the variable is lost.

Module scope

The same declaration statements used to create **Procedure** variables are also used to create **Module** variables inside a procedure. The difference between **Procedure level** variables and **Module level** variables is where they are declared. When you don't need global access to your variables, but you need them in more than one procedure, you can create a **Module** level variable. These variables are created by using the **Dim** or **Private** statements to declare the variable. These declarations must be placed in the (**General**) area of the **module** or **userform** where the variables are used.

Public Variables (Program Level)

Public variables have the broadest scope of all variables. In most programs, you will find that you need to have some variables available to all parts of the program. A **public variable** is recognized by every **module** in the active workbook. To create a variable that can be used anywhere in your program; you need to use the **Public** keyword in the declaration statement. These statements must be placed in the (**General**) area of a module and have the syntax:

> **Public** *variableName* [As type]

Allegheny Valley Institute of Technology ®

Authorized Training Programs

Exercise #4: Declaring Variables (by example)

1. In **Excel**, open a blank workbook.
2. Under the **Developer** tab, open the **Visual Basic Editor**, insert a **UserForm** and create the user interface with the **object names** shown below:

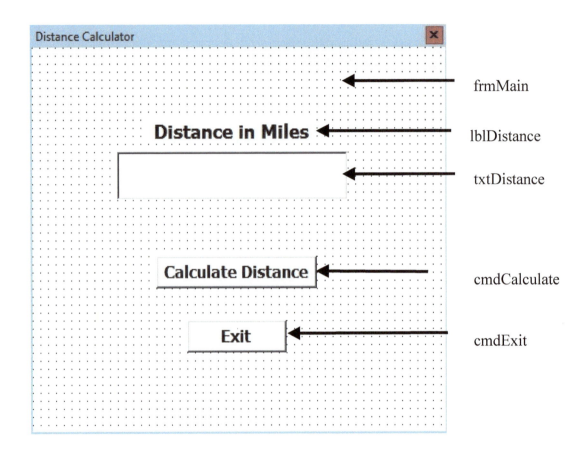

Select **File/Save** and save the workbook in your VBA Class folder as **DISTANCE** as a:

Excel Macro-Enabled Workbook

Allegheny Valley Institute of Technology ®

Authorized Training Programs

Double-click on the **Calculate Distance** button and enter the code below with comments:

```
Option Explicit

Private Sub cmdCalculate_Click()
    Dim intTime1 As Integer
    Dim intSpeed1 As Integer
    Dim intDistance As Integer

    intTime1 = 5                    'represents 5 hours
    intSpeed1 = 60                  'represents 60 mph
    intDistance = intSpeed1 * intTime1   'calculate the distance and place it in a variable called intDistance
    txtDistance.Text = intDistance       'display the calculated distance in the object called txtDistance

End Sub

Private Sub cmdExit_Click()
    End
End Sub
'
```

Save Your Work!

Answer the following questions:

1. Where can the "3" variables listed in the code above be used?

2. What are the limitations of this program?

3. What is the only way to calculate a new distance?

4. How can you keep the end-user from typing in the textbox?

5. What happens if you change variable **intDistance** to **Byte** and change the value of **intTime1** to **6**?

Allegheny Valley Institute of Technology ®

Authorized Training Programs

How to Manage Multiple UserForms

The easiest way to add an additional **userforms** to your project is to click **Insert/UserForm** on the **Menu** bar. It is always a good practice to name the **userform** right after you insert it.

Switching between forms in a multiple form project requires the use of "methods".

Remember from an earlier lecture, methods imply action of a particular object.

In general the syntax is:

ObjectName.Method

Syntax of each method:

- frmName.Hide   causes the userform to become invisible.
- frmName.Show   causes the userform to become visible.

Note: You have to use the **Hide** method before you can use the **Show** method.

Allegheny Valley Institute of Technology ®

Authorized Training Programs

Exercise #5: Using Multiple Forms in a Program (by example)

Note: Use Control + Enter to "text wrap" the caption of a command button.

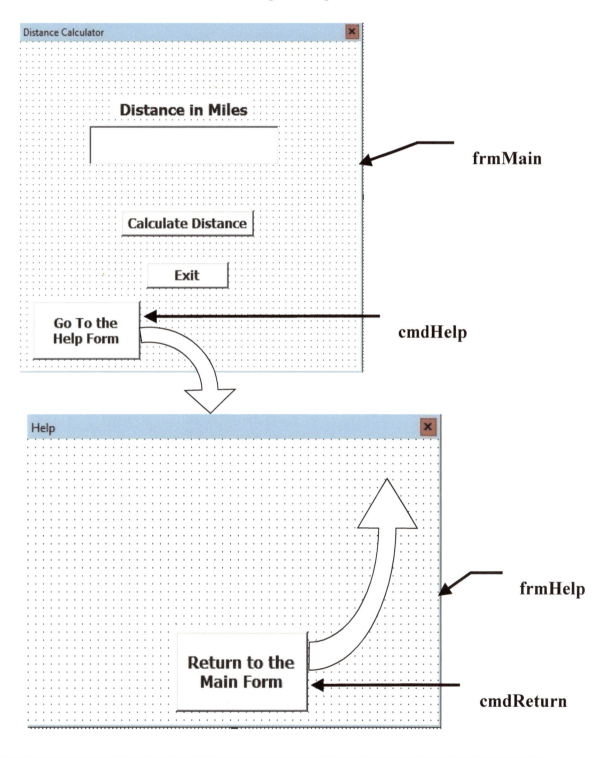

Allegheny Valley Institute of Technology ®

Authorized Training Programs

Notice the **Project** window in the upper left corner of your screen now has "2" userforms in it:

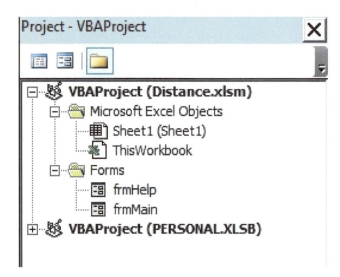

<u>Save and Close Your Work!</u>

Allegheny Valley Institute of Technology ®

Authorized Training Programs

Using VBA Modules

Modules are nothing more than containers for holding **VBA code**. *Modules* can contain declarations and procedures. VBA code that is placed in one or more *modules* can be "*called*" from any **Office** application to perform a specified task.

VBA Projects can be made up of:

- Objects
- Forms
- Modules

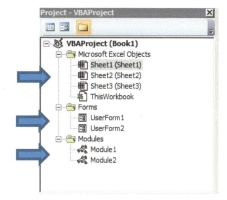

Allegheny Valley Institute of Technology ®

Authorized Training Programs

Understanding Modules and Projects in the Visual Basic Editor

It is important to understand how **Excel** organizes **VBA** code.

VBA code can be stored in modules, which in turn are stored in projects.

- A **module** is simply a collection of **VBA** code, such as procedures. A **module** can contain many procedures.
- A **project** is a collection of **modules**. There may be many modules in a project.

Each **Excel** workbook contains a single project. When you record a macro, **Excel** creates a module in the project for that workbook and puts the **VBA** code for the recorded macro into that module. If you record additional macros in the same **Excel** working session, those new macros will be stores in the same module. If you record additional macros the next time you run **Excel**, those macros will be recorded in a new module.

Modules are simply a way of organizing macros, and for now, it doesn't matter too much how many modules are in a given workbook's project, or how many macros are in any module.

VBA code can be typed and stored in the **VBA Editor** and placed in what are called *modules.*

- Every major **Microsoft Office** product has a **VBA Editor** and can use **VBA code** to control itself.

- The **VBA Editor** can be activated by pressing the **Alt + F11** keys in any **Microsoft Office** product.

Allegheny Valley Institute of Technology ®

Authorized Training Programs

General VBA Comments:

- To view a **module**, just double click on its icon in the **Project Explorer** window in the **VBA Editor**
  - For example, if you wanted to view the Module3 module then just double click on it with your mouse. A VBA module will resemble a **Word** document in both organization and typing.
  - A **VBA** module will appear in its own window within the **VBA Editor** when you double click on it to view it
  - A **VBA** module basically works like a **Word** document and follows the same basic typing rules

- You type code in a module then run it to control the program you want to control
  - For a program to be controlled with **VBA** it just has to be what is called VBA compatible. It does not have to be a Microsoft product
  - You can be in **Microsoft Excel** and control **Word** or **Access** or vice versa. Remember, it does not matter where the **VBA module** resides (i.e. what program), it is the code that controls whatever you are trying to command not its location.

- The code you type in a module comes from what can be referred to as a *library*
  - Programs expose their libraries to VBA allowing VBA to control them
  - Want to command a program, then reference its library in VBA then learn its commands so you can type them in your modules

- In **Microsoft Excel**, modules located under the **Modules** folder or **Classes** folder can be removed by right mouse clicking on their icons in the **Project Explorer** window and selecting **Remove**.
  - When removing a module, you have the choice to save it

Allegheny Valley Institute of Technology ®

Authorized Training Programs

Running VBA Code from a Module

As a beginner to **Excel VBA**, you might find it difficult to decide where to put your VBA code. So far, you have been shown how to run code by clicking a command button. This example teaches you how to **run code from a module**.

Exercise #6: Running VBA Code from a Module

1. File/Open   **Distance.xlsm**

2. Click the **Developer** tab and in the **Controls** group, select the **Insert** button.

3. In the **Form Controls** section, click the first control in the top-left called a "**Button**" and carefully drag a rectangle from the top-left corner of cell **L2** to the bottom-right corner of cell **M3**. The **Assign Macro** dialog box should appear:

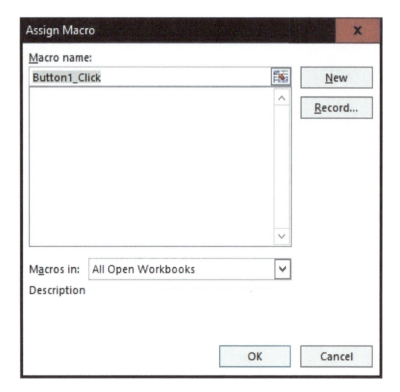

Allegheny Valley Institute of Technology ®

Authorized Training Programs

4. In the **Macro name** field, change the macro name to **Start_Click** and then click the **New** button.

5. In the newly created module sheet, type **frmMain.Show**

```
(General)

    Option Explicit

    Sub Start_Click()
        frmMain.Show
    End Sub
```

6. View the worksheet by clicking on the **Microsoft Excel** button in the upper left corner or pressing **ALT + F11**

7. Right-click the button and high-light the **Button1** text and change it to **Start**

8. Then make the button text 16 point, bold.

9. Then execute the **Start_Click** macro by clicking the **Start** button on the worksheet.

The instructor will show you how to execute the macro code from the ribbon by:

- Creating a **Tab** on the **Ribbon** called **My Macros**

- Creating a **Group** under **My Macros** called **Universal**

- Placing the **Distance** macro in the **Universal** group

Allegheny Valley Institute of Technology ®

Authorized Training Programs

Form Controls vs ActiveX Controls in VBA

Notice there are two different types of controls you can insert:

- Form Controls
- ActiveX Controls

What are Form Controls?

The **Form** controls are designed into **Excel** itself. **Form** Controls are objects which you can place onto an **Excel Worksheet** or **User Forms**, which give you the functionality to interact with your data.

You can use these controls to help select data. For example, drop-down boxes, list boxes, spinners, and scroll bars are useful for selecting items from a list. **Option Buttons** and **Check Boxes** allow selection of various options. **Buttons** allow execution of VBA code.

You can place form controls on user forms (created from **Visual Basic Editor**) or inside **Excel** worksheets.

By adding **form controls** to **user forms**, we can tell **Excel** how the value entered in that should be treated. This is done a special type of macros called as **Events**.

By adding a control to a worksheet and linking it to a cell, you can return a numeric value for the current position of the control. You can use that numeric value in conjunction with the **Offset**, **Index** or other worksheet functions to return values from lists.

.

What are Active-x Controls?

The **ActiveX** controls are loaded from separate **DLLs**. **Active X** controls are like **Form** controls on steroids in that they have a much wider range of properties than **Form Controls**.

They also have much better ties to VBA in terms of programmability and have a number of events that can be accessed programmatically.

The main limitation of **ActiveX** controls are that they use a Microsoft **ActiveX** component. This means that if you are sharing your workbook with an Apple Mac user using **Excel** for Mac these functions won't be available as **ActiveX** isn't available on that platform.

Allegheny Valley Institute of Technology ®

Authorized Training Programs

Creating VBA Macros using the Macro Recorder

Exercise #7 Using the Macro Recorder in Excel

> **Problem: Microsoft Excel** has many tools and shortcut keys, but there isn't a tool or shortcut for importing an **Access** database into **Excel,** format the data and filter the data on specific field headings.
>
> **Solution:** Use the macro recorder to record the steps needed to import an **Access** database into **Excel,** format the data and filter the data on specific field headings.

Recording the "AccessImport" Macro

1. Open **Microsoft Excel** with a blank worksheet.

2. Under the **Developer** tab, in the **Code** group, select the **Record Macro** button:

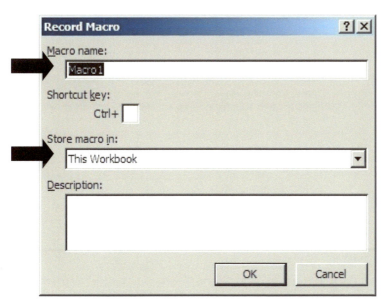

3. Change the **Macro name** to: **AccessImport**

4. Assign a shortcut key to be **Ctrl + i** (for import). <u>**Be careful, the shortcut key is case sensitive!**</u>

Allegheny Valley Institute of Technology ®

Authorized Training Programs

5. Select **This Workbook** for the macro to be stored in (we will discuss this in a moment)

6. Click **OK**. The **Record Marco** button will replace the **Stop Recording** button.

7. Under the **Data** tab, in the **Get & Transform Data** group, click **Get Data / From Database / From Microsoft Access Database** and find the **Northwind.accdb** file on your desktop. Select it and click the **Import** button.

8. Select the **Employees Extended** table and click the **Load** button.

Your screen should look like:

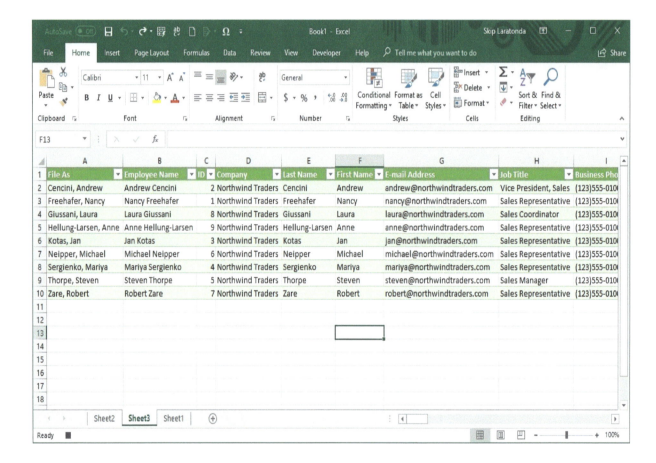

Allegheny Valley Institute of Technology ®

Authorized Training Programs

Notice that the information in column **A** is redundant with column's **E** and **F**!

9. Delete both column's **E** and **F**.

10. Select the entire worksheet and make everything 12 point.

11. Under the heading **Job Title**, filter for only the **Sales Representative's**.

12. Then under the heading **City**, filter for only **Seattle**.

Your screen should look like:

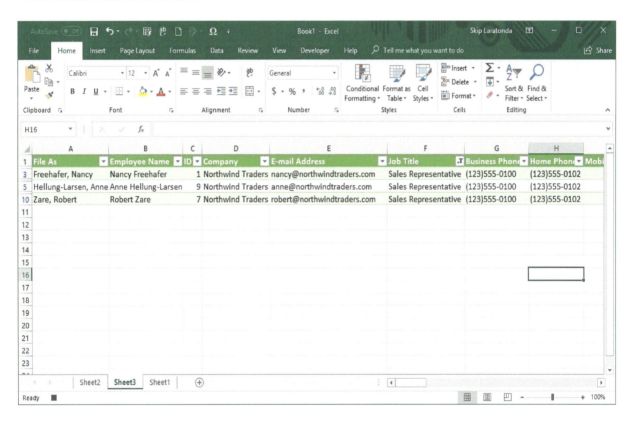

13. As a final step in your macro code, just for fun, select cell **A3**.

14. Turn off the recorder by clicking the **Stop Recording** button under the **Developer** tab.

Allegheny Valley Institute of Technology ®
Authorized Training Programs

To View the "AccessImport" Macro Procedure

In **Office 2016**, Excel macros are stored in separate "module sheets" in **Module** folders that are part of the workbook you were in when you created the macro. Excel stores macros invisibly within the workbook in project "modules". The only way to see the VB code is by using the **Visual Basic Editor.**

To view the "AccessImport" macro:

1. Under the **Developer** tab, in the **Code** group, click the **Visual Basic** button or press Alt + F11(toggles)

2. In the **Project** window, double-click the **Modules** folder and double-click **Module1**.

   Notice the Visual Basic code that was generated for you.

Answer the following questions:

   1. Where in the code did VBA find the **Access** database **Northwind.accdb**?

   2. Where in the code did VBA add a new worksheet when it imported the database?

   3. Where in the code did VBA delete columns **E** and **F**?

   4. Where in the code did VBA make all cells in the worksheet **12pt**?

   5. Where in the code did VBA filter the data for *Sales Representative*?

   6. Where in the code did VBA preform the final step of selecting cell **A3**?

Allegheny Valley Institute of Technology ®
Authorized Training Programs

Where are Macros Stored?

As mentioned before, your macros are stored invisibly in project modules within the workbook they were created in. This, however, is only true if you allow **Excel** to use the default **"This workbook"** selection.

They are actually "3" places where these macro projects can be stored:

> **This Workbook** - This is the default selection. The macro you are about to create will be stored in, and saved with, the workbook you are currently using.

> **New Workbook** - A workbook is opened and the macro procedure is stored in this new workbook.

> **Personal Macro Workbook** - The **Personal Macro Workbook** is the only macro workbook that always opens when you start Excel. This workbook is useful for storing Sub and Function procedures (macros) that you use frequently and always want loaded. Because the **Personal Macro Workbook**, PERSONAL.XLS, is saved by **Excel** in the **XLSTART** directory, this workbook loads automatically when **Excel** starts.

> You normally cannot see the **Personal Macro Workbook** because it is hidden.

Notes:

1. Many *macro procedures* can be stored on a single module sheet.

2. *Macro procedures* cannot run without the workbook in which they were stored open. Therefore consider storing useful macros in the "Personal Macro Workbook".

Allegheny Valley Institute of Technology ®

Authorized Training Programs

This information describes the use of the Personal Macro Workbook for recording, writing and editing Microsoft Visual Basic for Applications (VBA) macros.

1. **What is the Personal Macro Workbook?**

   The **Personal Macro Workbook** is a file where you can save frequently used macros, and code modules so that you can call them from any workbook in **Excel**.

2. **How do I Create the Personal Macro Workbook?**

   The **Personal Macro Workbook** does not get created until you run the macro recorder for the first time and choose to save the macro in the **Personal Macro Workbook**. The easiest way to create the **Personal Macro Workbook** is to record a "dummy" macro. To do this, follow these steps:

   a. Start **Excel** so that only a new workbook is open. On the **Developer** tab, click the **Record Macro** button.

   b. In the **Record Macro** dialog box, click **Personal Macro Workbook** in the **Store macro in list**.

   c. Click **OK**. Because you are creating a "dummy" macro, do not click or type anything.

   d. On the **Developer** tab, click the **Stop Recording** button.

   e. You do not have to save the workbook but when asked if you want to save the **Personal Macro Workbook** make sure to save it.

   When you start Excel, this **Personal Macro Workbook** opens as a hidden workbook.

   Any time you create a new macro and save it in your personal workbook or update any macros that it contains, you are prompted to save the personal workbook just as it did the first time you saved it.

Allegheny Valley Institute of Technology ®
Authorized Training Programs

3. **Where is the Excel Personal Macro Workbook Located?**

C:\Users\Your Username\AppData\Roaming\Microsoft\Excel\ XLSTART\ PERSONAL.XLSB

4. **Why do I need the Personal Macro Workbook?**

When you first create a macro in a workbook, it works only in that workbook. But what if you want to use the macro in other workbooks? To make your macros available every time you open Excel, create them in a workbook called the **Personal Macro Workbook**. The **Personal Macro Workbook** is a hidden workbook stored on your computer, which opens every time you open **Excel**.

5. **How do I unhide the Personal Macro Workbook once it is created?**

Any macros you save to the **Personal Macro Workbook** can be edited only by first unhiding the **Personal Macro Workbook**. When you start **Excel**, the **Personal Macro Workbook** is loaded but you can't see it because it's hidden. To see it:

   a. Click **View > Unhide**.
   b. In the **Unhide** dialog box, you should see **PERSONAL.XLSB**.
   c. Click **OK** to view the personal workbook.
   d. To hide the personal workbook, make sure you have **Personal.xlsb** selected, and then click **Hide** on the **View** tab.

EFL8/18/2018

Allegheny Valley Institute of Technology ®
Authorized Training Programs